Short Story Writing Journal

Dedication

This Short Story Writing Journal Book is dedicated to all the writing enthusiasts out there who want to keep their short stories notes organized and document their findings in the process.

You are my inspiration for producing books and I'm honored to be a part of keeping all of your Short Story notes and records organized.

This journal notebook will help you record the details of your stories.

Thoughtfully put together with these sections to record: Title, Themes, Protagonist, Get Writing, and Word Count.

How to Use this Book

The purpose of this book is to keep all of your Short Story notes all in one place. It will help keep you organized.

This Short Story Writing Journal Book will allow you to accurately document details about your short stories.

Here are examples of the prompts for you to fill in and write about your experience in this book:

1. Title - Write your title.
2. Themes - Record Prompt, Setting, Thoughts, and Message.
3. Protagonist - Log Name, Driving Goal, and Obstacle or Conflict ideas.
4. Get Writing - Blank lined space to write your short story.
5. Word Count - Write the number of words in your story.

Title

Themes

Prompt

Setting

Message

Protagonist

Name

Driving Goal

Obstacle or Conflict

Get writing!

Word Count

Title

Themes

Prompt

Setting

Message

Protagonist

Name

Driving Goal

Obstacle or Conflict

Get writing!

Word Count

Title

Themes

Prompt

Setting

Message

Protagonist

Name

Driving Goal

Obstacle or Conflict

Get writing!

Word Count

Title

Themes

Prompt

Setting

Message

Protagonist

Name

Driving Goal

Obstacle or Conflict

Get writing!

Word Count

Title

Themes

Prompt

Setting

Message

Protagonist

Name

Driving Goal

Obstacle or Conflict

Get writing!

Word Count ____________

Title

Themes

Prompt

Setting

Message

Protagonist

Name

Driving Goal

Obstacle or Conflict

Get writing!

Word Count

Title

Themes

Prompt

Setting

Message

Protagonist

Name

Driving Goal

Obstacle or Conflict

Get writing!

Word Count

Title

Themes

Prompt

Setting

Message

Protagonist

Name

Driving Goal

Obstacle or Conflict

Get writing!

Word Count ____________

Title

Themes

Prompt

Setting

Message

Protagonist

Name

Driving Goal

Obstacle or Conflict

Get writing!

Word Count

Title

Themes

Prompt

Setting

Message

Protagonist

Name

Driving Goal

Obstacle or Conflict

Get writing!

Word Count

Title

Themes

Prompt

Setting

Message

Protagonist

Name

Driving Goal

Obstacle or Conflict

Get writing!

Word Count

Title

Themes

Prompt

Setting

Message

Protagonist

Name

Driving Goal

Obstacle or Conflict

Get writing!

Word Count

Title

Themes

Prompt

Setting

Message

Protagonist

Name

Driving Goal

Obstacle or Conflict

Get writing!

Word Count

Title

Themes

Prompt

Setting

Message

Protagonist

Name

Driving Goal

Obstacle or Conflict

Get writing!

Word Count

Title

Themes

Prompt

Setting

Message

Protagonist

Name

Driving Goal

Obstacle or Conflict

Get writing!

Word Count

Title

Themes

Prompt

Setting

Message

Protagonist

Name

Driving Goal

Obstacle or Conflict

Get writing!

Word Count

Title

Themes

Prompt

Setting

Message

Protagonist

Name

Driving Goal

Obstacle or Conflict

Get writing!

Word Count

Title

Themes

Prompt

Setting

Message

Protagonist

Name

Driving Goal

Obstacle or Conflict

Get writing!

Word Count

Title

Themes

Prompt

Setting

Message

Protagonist

Name

Driving Goal

Obstacle or Conflict

Get writing!

Word Count

Title

Themes

Prompt

Setting

Message

Protagonist

Name

Driving Goal

Obstacle or Conflict

Get writing!

Word Count ____________

Title

Themes

Prompt

Setting

Message

Protagonist

Name

Driving Goal

Obstacle or Conflict

Get writing!

Word Count

Title

Themes

Prompt

Setting

Message

Protagonist

Name

Driving Goal

Obstacle or Conflict

Get writing!

Word Count

Title

Themes

Prompt

Setting

Message

Protagonist

Name

Driving Goal

Obstacle or Conflict

Get writing!

Word Count

Title

Themes

Prompt

Setting

Message

Protagonist

Name

Driving Goal

Obstacle or Conflict

Get writing!

Word Count ____________

Title

Themes

Prompt

Setting

Message

Protagonist

Name

Driving Goal

Obstacle or Conflict

Get writing!

Word Count

Title

Themes

Prompt

Setting

Message

Protagonist

Name

Driving Goal

Obstacle or Conflict

Get writing!

Word Count

Title

Themes

Prompt

Setting

Message

Protagonist

Name

Driving Goal

Obstacle or Conflict

Get writing!

Word Count

Title

Themes

Prompt

Setting

Message

Protagonist

Name

Driving Goal

Obstacle or Conflict

Get writing!

Word Count

Title

Themes

Prompt

Setting

Message

Protagonist

Name

Driving Goal

Obstacle or Conflict

Get writing!

Word Count

Title

Themes

Prompt

Setting

Message

Protagonist

Name

Driving Goal

Obstacle or Conflict

Get writing!

Word Count

Title

Themes

Prompt

Setting

Message

Protagonist

Name

Driving Goal

Obstacle or Conflict

Get writing!

Word Count

Title

Themes

Prompt

Setting

Message

Protagonist

Name

Driving Goal

Obstacle or Conflict

Get writing!

Word Count

Title

Themes

Prompt

Setting

Message

Protagonist

Name

Driving Goal

Obstacle or Conflict

Get writing!

Word Count ____________

Title

Themes

Prompt

Setting

Message

Protagonist

Name

Driving Goal

Obstacle or Conflict

Get writing!

Word Count ____________

Title

Themes

Prompt

Setting

Message

Protagonist

Name

Driving Goal

Obstacle or Conflict

Get writing!

Word Count

Title

Themes

Prompt

Setting

Message

Protagonist

Name

Driving Goal

Obstacle or Conflict

Get writing!

Word Count

Title

Themes

Prompt

Setting

Message

Protagonist

Name

Driving Goal

Obstacle or Conflict

Get writing!

Word Count

Title

Themes

Prompt

Setting

Message

Protagonist

Name

Driving Goal

Obstacle or Conflict

Get writing!

Word Count

Title

Themes

Prompt

Setting

Message

Protagonist

Name

Driving Goal

Obstacle or Conflict

Get writing!

Word Count

Title

Themes

Prompt

Setting

Message

Protagonist

Name

Driving Goal

Obstacle or Conflict

Get writing!

Word Count

Title

Themes

Prompt

Setting

Message

Protagonist

Name

Driving Goal

Obstacle or Conflict

Get writing!

Word Count

Title

Themes

Prompt

Setting

Message

Protagonist

Name

Driving Goal

Obstacle or Conflict

Get writing!

Word Count

Title

Themes

Prompt

Setting

Message

Protagonist

Name

Driving Goal

Obstacle or Conflict

Get writing!

Word Count

Title

Themes

Prompt

Setting

Message

Protagonist

Name

Driving Goal

Obstacle or Conflict

Get writing!

Word Count

Title

Themes

Prompt

Setting

Message

Protagonist

Name

Driving Goal

Obstacle or Conflict

Get writing!

Word Count

Title

Themes

Prompt

Setting

Message

Protagonist

Name

Driving Goal

Obstacle or Conflict

Get writing!

Word Count

Title

Themes

Prompt

Setting

Message

Protagonist

Name

Driving Goal

Obstacle or Conflict

Get writing!

Word Count

Title

Themes

Prompt

Setting

Message

Protagonist

Name

Driving Goal

Obstacle or Conflict

Get writing!

Word Count

Title

Themes

Prompt

Setting

Message

Protagonist

Name

Driving Goal

Obstacle or Conflict

Get writing!

Word Count

Title

Themes

Prompt

Setting

Message

Protagonist

Name

Driving Goal

Obstacle or Conflict

Get writing!

Word Count

Title

Themes

Prompt

Setting

Message

Protagonist

Name

Driving Goal

Obstacle or Conflict

Get writing!

Word Count

Title

Themes

Prompt

Setting

Message

Protagonist

Name

Driving Goal

Obstacle or Conflict

Get writing!

Word Count

Title

Themes

Prompt

Setting

Message

Protagonist

Name

Driving Goal

Obstacle or Conflict

Get writing!

Word Count

Title

Themes

Prompt

Setting

Message

Protagonist

Name

Driving Goal

Obstacle or Conflict

Get writing!

Word Count

Title

Themes

Prompt

Setting

Message

Protagonist

Name

Driving Goal

Obstacle or Conflict

Get writing!

Word Count

Title

Themes

Prompt

Setting

Message

Protagonist

Name

Driving Goal

Obstacle or Conflict

Get writing!

Word Count

Title

Themes

Prompt

Setting

Message

Protagonist

Name

Driving Goal

Obstacle or Conflict

Get writing!

Word Count

Title

Themes

Prompt

Setting

Message

Protagonist

Name

Driving Goal

Obstacle or Conflict

Get writing!

Word Count

Title

Themes

Prompt

Setting

Message

Protagonist

Name

Driving Goal

Obstacle or Conflict

Get writing!

Word Count

Title

Themes

Prompt

Setting

Message

Protagonist

Name

Driving Goal

Obstacle or Conflict

Get writing!

Word Count

Title

Themes

Prompt

Setting

Message

Protagonist

Name

Driving Goal

Obstacle or Conflict

Get writing!

Word Count

Title

Themes

Prompt

Setting

Message

Protagonist

Name

Driving Goal

Obstacle or Conflict

Get writing!

Word Count

Title

Themes

Prompt

Setting

Message

Protagonist

Name

Driving Goal

Obstacle or Conflict

Get writing!

Word Count

Title

Themes

Prompt

Setting

Message

Protagonist

Name

Driving Goal

Obstacle or Conflict

Get writing!

Word Count ____________

Title

Themes

Prompt

Setting

Message

Protagonist

Name

Driving Goal

Obstacle or Conflict

Get writing!

Word Count

Title

Themes

Prompt

Setting

Message

Protagonist

Name

Driving Goal

Obstacle or Conflict

Get writing!

Word Count

Title

Themes

Prompt

Setting

Message

Protagonist

Name

Driving Goal

Obstacle or Conflict

Get writing!

Word Count

Title

Themes

Prompt

Setting

Message

Protagonist

Name

Driving Goal

Obstacle or Conflict

Get writing!

Word Count

Title

Themes

Prompt

Setting

Message

Protagonist

Name

Driving Goal

Obstacle or Conflict

Get writing!

Word Count

Title

Themes

Prompt

Setting

Message

Protagonist

Name

Driving Goal

Obstacle or Conflict

Get writing!

Word Count

Title

Themes

Prompt

Setting

Message

Protagonist

Name

Driving Goal

Obstacle or Conflict

Get writing!

Word Count ______________

Title

Themes

Prompt

Setting

Message

Protagonist

Name

Driving Goal

Obstacle or Conflict

Get writing!

Word Count

Title

Themes

Prompt

Setting

Message

Protagonist

Name

Driving Goal

Obstacle or Conflict

Get writing!

Word Count

Title

Themes

Prompt

Setting

Message

Protagonist

Name

Driving Goal

Obstacle or Conflict

Get writing!

Word Count ____________

Title

Themes

Prompt

Setting

Message

Protagonist

Name

Driving Goal

Obstacle or Conflict

Get writing!

Word Count

Title

Themes

Prompt

Setting

Message

Protagonist

Name

Driving Goal

Obstacle or Conflict

Get writing!

Word Count

Title

Themes

Prompt

Setting

Message

Protagonist

Name

Driving Goal

Obstacle or Conflict

Get writing!

Word Count

Title

Themes

Prompt

Setting

Message

Protagonist

Name

Driving Goal

Obstacle or Conflict

Get writing!

Word Count

Title

Themes

Prompt

Setting

Message

Protagonist

Name

Driving Goal

Obstacle or Conflict

Get writing!

Word Count

Title

Themes

Prompt

Setting

Message

Protagonist

Name

Driving Goal

Obstacle or Conflict

Get writing!

Word Count ____________

Title

Themes

Prompt

Setting

Message

Protagonist

Name

Driving Goal

Obstacle or Conflict

Get writing!

Word Count

Title

Themes

Prompt

Setting

Message

Protagonist

Name

Driving Goal

Obstacle or Conflict

Get writing!

Word Count

Title

Themes

Prompt

Setting

Message

Protagonist

Name

Driving Goal

Obstacle or Conflict

Get writing!

Word Count

Title

Themes

Prompt

Setting

Message

Protagonist

Name

Driving Goal

Obstacle or Conflict

Get writing!

Word Count

Title

Themes

Prompt

Setting

Message

Protagonist

Name

Driving Goal

Obstacle or Conflict

Get writing!

Word Count

Title

Themes

Prompt

Setting

Message

Protagonist

Name

Driving Goal

Obstacle or Conflict

Get writing!

Word Count

Title

Themes

Prompt

Setting

Message

Protagonist

Name

Driving Goal

Obstacle or Conflict

Get writing!

Word Count

Title

Themes

Prompt

Setting

Message

Protagonist

Name

Driving Goal

Obstacle or Conflict

Get writing!

Word Count

Title

Themes

Prompt

Setting

Message

Protagonist

Name

Driving Goal

Obstacle or Conflict

Get writing!

Word Count

Title

Themes

Prompt

Setting

Message

Protagonist

Name

Driving Goal

Obstacle or Conflict

Get writing!

Word Count

Title

Themes

Prompt

Setting

Message

Protagonist

Name

Driving Goal

Obstacle or Conflict

Get writing!

Word Count

Title

Themes

Prompt

Setting

Message

Protagonist

Name

Driving Goal

Obstacle or Conflict

Get writing!

Word Count

Title

Themes

Prompt

Setting

Message

Protagonist

Name

Driving Goal

Obstacle or Conflict

Get writing!

Word Count

Title

Themes

Prompt

Setting

Message

Protagonist

Name

Driving Goal

Obstacle or Conflict

Get writing!

Word Count

Title

Themes

Prompt

Setting

Message

Protagonist

Name

Driving Goal

Obstacle or Conflict

Get writing!

Word Count

Title

Themes

Prompt

Setting

Message

Protagonist

Name

Driving Goal

Obstacle or Conflict

Get writing!

Word Count

Title

Themes

Prompt

Setting

Message

Protagonist

Name

Driving Goal

Obstacle or Conflict

Get writing!

Word Count

Title

Themes

Prompt

Setting

Message

Protagonist

Name

Driving Goal

Obstacle or Conflict

Get writing!

Word Count

Title

Themes

Prompt

Setting

Message

Protagonist

Name

Driving Goal

Obstacle or Conflict

Get writing!

Word Count

Title

Themes

Prompt

Setting

Message

Protagonist

Name

Driving Goal

Obstacle or Conflict

Get writing!

Word Count

Title

Themes

Prompt

Setting

Message

Protagonist

Name

Driving Goal

Obstacle or Conflict

Get writing!

Word Count

Title

Themes

Prompt

Setting

Message

Protagonist

Name

Driving Goal

Obstacle or Conflict

Get writing!

Word Count

Title

Themes

Prompt

Setting

Message

Protagonist

Name

Driving Goal

Obstacle or Conflict

Get writing!

Word Count

Title

Themes

Prompt

Setting

Message

Protagonist

Name

Driving Goal

Obstacle or Conflict

Get writing!

Word Count

Title

Themes

Prompt

Setting

Message

Protagonist

Name

Driving Goal

Obstacle or Conflict

Get writing!

Word Count

Title

Themes

Prompt

Setting

Message

Protagonist

Name

Driving Goal

Obstacle or Conflict

Get writing!

Word Count

Title

Themes

Prompt

Setting

Message

Protagonist

Name

Driving Goal

Obstacle or Conflict

Get writing!

Word Count

Title

Themes

Prompt

Setting

Message

Protagonist

Name

Driving Goal

Obstacle or Conflict

Get writing!

Word Count ______________

Title

Themes

Prompt

Setting

Message

Protagonist

Name

Driving Goal

Obstacle or Conflict

Get writing!

Word Count

Title

Themes

Prompt

Setting

Message

Protagonist

Name

Driving Goal

Obstacle or Conflict

Get writing!

Word Count

Title

Themes

Prompt

Setting

Message

Protagonist

Name

Driving Goal

Obstacle or Conflict

Get writing!

Word Count

Title

Themes

Prompt

Setting

Message

Protagonist

Name

Driving Goal

Obstacle or Conflict

Get writing!

Word Count

Title

Themes

Prompt

Setting

Message

Protagonist

Name

Driving Goal

Obstacle or Conflict

Get writing!

Word Count

Title

Themes

Prompt

Setting

Message

Protagonist

Name

Driving Goal

Obstacle or Conflict

Get writing!

Word Count

Title

Themes

Prompt

Setting

Message

Protagonist

Name

Driving Goal

Obstacle or Conflict

Get writing!

Word Count

Title

Themes

Prompt

Setting

Message

Protagonist

Name

Driving Goal

Obstacle or Conflict

Get writing!

Word Count

Title

Themes

Prompt

Setting

Message

Protagonist

Name

Driving Goal

Obstacle or Conflict

Get writing!

Word Count

Title

Themes

Prompt

Setting

Message

Protagonist

Name

Driving Goal

Obstacle or Conflict

Get writing!

Word Count

Title

Themes

Prompt

Setting

Message

Protagonist

Name

Driving Goal

Obstacle or Conflict

Get writing!

Word Count

Title

Themes

Prompt

Setting

Message

Protagonist

Name

Driving Goal

Obstacle or Conflict

Get writing!

Word Count

Title

Themes

Prompt

Setting

Message

Protagonist

Name

Driving Goal

Obstacle or Conflict

Get writing!

Word Count

Title

Themes

Prompt

Setting

Message

Protagonist

Name

Driving Goal

Obstacle or Conflict

Get writing!

Word Count

Title

Themes

Prompt

Setting

Message

Protagonist

Name

Driving Goal

Obstacle or Conflict

Get writing!

Word Count

Title

Themes

Prompt

Setting

Message

Protagonist

Name

Driving Goal

Obstacle or Conflict

Get writing!

Word Count

Title

Themes

Prompt

Setting

Message

Protagonist

Name

Driving Goal

Obstacle or Conflict

Get writing!

Word Count ____________

Title

Themes

Prompt

Setting

Message

Protagonist

Name

Driving Goal

Obstacle or Conflict

Get writing!

Word Count

Title

Themes

Prompt

Setting

Message

Protagonist

Name

Driving Goal

Obstacle or Conflict

Get writing!

Word Count

Title

Themes

Prompt

Setting

Message

Protagonist

Name

Driving Goal

Obstacle or Conflict

Get writing!

Word Count

Title

Themes

Prompt

Setting

Message

Protagonist

Name

Driving Goal

Obstacle or Conflict

Get writing!

Word Count

Title

Themes

Prompt

Setting

Message

Protagonist

Name

Driving Goal

Obstacle or Conflict

Get writing!

Word Count

Title

Themes

Prompt

Setting

Message

Protagonist

Name

Driving Goal

Obstacle or Conflict

Get writing!

Word Count

Title

Themes

Prompt

Setting

Message

Protagonist

Name

Driving Goal

Obstacle or Conflict

Get writing!

Word Count

Title

Themes

Prompt

Setting

Message

Protagonist

Name

Driving Goal

Obstacle or Conflict

Get writing!

Word Count

Title

Themes

Prompt

Setting

Message

Protagonist

Name

Driving Goal

Obstacle or Conflict

Get writing!

Word Count

Title

Themes

Prompt

Setting

Message

Protagonist

Name

Driving Goal

Obstacle or Conflict

Get writing!

Word Count

Title

Themes

Prompt

Setting

Message

Protagonist

Name

Driving Goal

Obstacle or Conflict

Get writing!

Word Count

Title

Themes

Prompt

Setting

Message

Protagonist

Name

Driving Goal

Obstacle or Conflict

Get writing!

Word Count

Title

Themes

Prompt

Setting

Message

Protagonist

Name

Driving Goal

Obstacle or Conflict

Get writing!

Word Count ____________

Title

Themes

Prompt

Setting

Message

Protagonist

Name

Driving Goal

Obstacle or Conflict

Get writing!

Word Count

Title

Themes

Prompt

Setting

Message

Protagonist

Name

Driving Goal

Obstacle or Conflict

Get writing!

Word Count

Title

Themes

Prompt

Setting

Message

Protagonist

Name

Driving Goal

Obstacle or Conflict

Get writing!

Word Count

Title

Themes

Prompt

Setting

Message

Protagonist

Name

Driving Goal

Obstacle or Conflict

Get writing!

Word Count

Title

Themes

Prompt

Setting

Message

Protagonist

Name

Driving Goal

Obstacle or Conflict

Get writing!

Word Count

Title

Themes

Prompt

Setting

Message

Protagonist

Name

Driving Goal

Obstacle or Conflict

Get writing!

Word Count

Title

Themes

Prompt

Setting

Message

Protagonist

Name

Driving Goal

Obstacle or Conflict

Get writing!

Word Count

Title

Themes

Prompt

Setting

Message

Protagonist

Name

Driving Goal

Obstacle or Conflict

Get writing!

Word Count

Title

Themes

Prompt

Setting

Message

Protagonist

Name

Driving Goal

Obstacle or Conflict

Get writing!

Word Count

Title

Themes

Prompt

Setting

Message

Protagonist

Name

Driving Goal

Obstacle or Conflict

Get writing!

Word Count

Title

Themes

Prompt

Setting

Message

Protagonist

Name

Driving Goal

Obstacle or Conflict

Get writing!

Word Count

Title

Themes

Prompt

Setting

Message

Protagonist

Name

Driving Goal

Obstacle or Conflict

Get writing!

Word Count

Title

Themes

Prompt

Setting

Message

Protagonist

Name

Driving Goal

Obstacle or Conflict

Get writing!

Word Count

Title

Themes

Prompt

Setting

Message

Protagonist

Name

Driving Goal

Obstacle or Conflict

Get writing!

Word Count

Title

Themes

Prompt

Setting

Message

Protagonist

Name

Driving Goal

Obstacle or Conflict

Get writing!

Word Count

Title

Themes

Prompt

Setting

Message

Protagonist

Name

Driving Goal

Obstacle or Conflict

Get writing!

Word Count ____________

Title

Themes

Prompt

Setting

Message

Protagonist

Name

Driving Goal

Obstacle or Conflict

Get writing!

Word Count

Title

Themes

Prompt

Setting

Message

Protagonist

Name

Driving Goal

Obstacle or Conflict

Get writing!

Word Count

Title

Themes

Prompt

Setting

Message

Protagonist

Name

Driving Goal

Obstacle or Conflict

Get writing!

Word Count

Title

Themes

Prompt

Setting

Message

Protagonist

Name

Driving Goal

Obstacle or Conflict

Get writing!

Word Count

Title

Themes

Prompt

Setting

Message

Protagonist

Name

Driving Goal

Obstacle or Conflict

Get writing!

Word Count

Title

Themes

Prompt

Setting

Message

Protagonist

Name

Driving Goal

Obstacle or Conflict

Get writing!

Word Count

Title

Themes

Prompt

Setting

Message

Protagonist

Name

Driving Goal

Obstacle or Conflict

Get writing!

Word Count

Title

Themes

Prompt

Setting

Message

Protagonist

Name

Driving Goal

Obstacle or Conflict

Get writing!

Word Count

Title

Themes

Prompt

Setting

Message

Protagonist

Name

Driving Goal

Obstacle or Conflict

Get writing!

Word Count

Title

Themes

Prompt

Setting

Message

Protagonist

Name

Driving Goal

Obstacle or Conflict

Get writing!

Word Count ____________

Title

Themes

Prompt

Setting

Message

Protagonist

Name

Driving Goal

Obstacle or Conflict

Get writing!

Word Count

Title

Themes

Prompt

Setting

Message

Protagonist

Name

Driving Goal

Obstacle or Conflict

Get writing!

Word Count

Title

Themes

Prompt

Setting

Message

Protagonist

Name

Driving Goal

Obstacle or Conflict

Get writing!

Word Count

Title

Themes

Prompt

Setting

Message

Protagonist

Name

Driving Goal

Obstacle or Conflict

Get writing!

Word Count

Title

Themes

Prompt

Setting

Message

Protagonist

Name

Driving Goal

Obstacle or Conflict

Get writing!

Word Count

Title

Themes

Prompt

Setting

Message

Protagonist

Name

Driving Goal

Obstacle or Conflict

Get writing!

Word Count

Title

Themes

Prompt

Setting

Message

Protagonist

Name

Driving Goal

Obstacle or Conflict

Get writing!

Word Count

Title

Themes

Prompt

Setting

Message

Protagonist

Name

Driving Goal

Obstacle or Conflict

Get writing!

Word Count

Title

Themes

Prompt

Setting

Message

Protagonist

Name

Driving Goal

Obstacle or Conflict

Get writing!

Word Count

Title

Themes

Prompt

Setting

Message

Protagonist

Name

Driving Goal

Obstacle or Conflict

Get writing!

Word Count

Title

Themes

Prompt

Setting

Message

Protagonist

Name

Driving Goal

Obstacle or Conflict

Get writing!

Word Count

Title

Themes

Prompt

Setting

Message

Protagonist

Name

Driving Goal

Obstacle or Conflict

Get writing!

Word Count

Title

Themes

Prompt

Setting

Message

Protagonist

Name

Driving Goal

Obstacle or Conflict

Get writing!

Word Count

Title

Themes

Prompt

Setting

Message

Protagonist

Name

Driving Goal

Obstacle or Conflict

Get writing!

Word Count

Title

Themes

Prompt

Setting

Message

Protagonist

Name

Driving Goal

Obstacle or Conflict

Get writing!

Word Count

Title

Themes

Prompt

Setting

Message

Protagonist

Name

Driving Goal

Obstacle or Conflict

Get writing!

Word Count

Title

Themes

Prompt

Setting

Message

Protagonist

Name

Driving Goal

Obstacle or Conflict

Get writing!

Word Count

Title

Themes

Prompt

Setting

Message

Protagonist

Name

Driving Goal

Obstacle or Conflict

Get writing!

Word Count

Title

Themes

Prompt

Setting

Message

Protagonist

Name

Driving Goal

Obstacle or Conflict

Get writing!

Word Count

Title

Themes

Prompt

Setting

Message

Protagonist

Name

Driving Goal

Obstacle or Conflict

Get writing!

Word Count

Title

Themes

Prompt

Setting

Message

Protagonist

Name

Driving Goal

Obstacle or Conflict

Get writing!

Word Count

Title

Themes

Prompt

Setting

Message

Protagonist

Name

Driving Goal

Obstacle or Conflict

Get writing!

Word Count

Title

Themes

Prompt

Setting

Message

Protagonist

Name

Driving Goal

Obstacle or Conflict

Get writing!

Word Count

Title

Themes

Prompt

Setting

Message

Protagonist

Name

Driving Goal

Obstacle or Conflict

Get writing!

Word Count

Title

Themes

Prompt

Setting

Message

Protagonist

Name

Driving Goal

Obstacle or Conflict

Get writing!

Word Count

Title

Themes

Prompt

Setting

Message

Protagonist

Name

Driving Goal

Obstacle or Conflict

Get writing!

Word Count

Title

Themes

Prompt

Setting

Message

Protagonist

Name

Driving Goal

Obstacle or Conflict

Get writing!

Word Count

Title

Themes

Prompt

Setting

Message

Protagonist

Name

Driving Goal

Obstacle or Conflict

Get writing!

Word Count

Title

Themes

Prompt

Setting

Message

Protagonist

Name

Driving Goal

Obstacle or Conflict

Get writing!

Word Count

Title

Themes

Prompt

Setting

Message

Protagonist

Name

Driving Goal

Obstacle or Conflict

Get writing!

Word Count

Title

Themes

Prompt

Setting

Message

Protagonist

Name

Driving Goal

Obstacle or Conflict

Get writing!

Word Count

Title

Themes

Prompt

Setting

Message

Protagonist

Name

Driving Goal

Obstacle or Conflict

Get writing!

Word Count

Title

Themes

Prompt

Setting

Message

Protagonist

Name

Driving Goal

Obstacle or Conflict

Get writing!

Word Count ____________

Title

Themes

Prompt

Setting

Message

Protagonist

Name

Driving Goal

Obstacle or Conflict

Get writing!

Word Count

Title

Themes

Prompt

Setting

Message

Protagonist

Name

Driving Goal

Obstacle or Conflict

Get writing!

Word Count

Title

Themes

Prompt

Setting

Message

Protagonist

Name

Driving Goal

Obstacle or Conflict

Get writing!

Word Count

Title

Themes

Prompt

Setting

Message

Protagonist

Name

Driving Goal

Obstacle or Conflict

Get writing!

Word Count

Title

Themes

Prompt

Setting

Message

Protagonist

Name

Driving Goal

Obstacle or Conflict

Get writing!

Word Count

Title

Themes

Prompt

Setting

Message

Protagonist

Name

Driving Goal

Obstacle or Conflict

Get writing!

Word Count

Title

Themes

Prompt

Setting

Message

Protagonist

Name

Driving Goal

Obstacle or Conflict

Get writing!

Word Count

Title

Themes

Prompt

Setting

Message

Protagonist

Name

Driving Goal

Obstacle or Conflict

Get writing!

Word Count

Title

Themes

Prompt

Setting

Message

Protagonist

Name

Driving Goal

Obstacle or Conflict

Get writing!

Word Count

Title

Themes

Prompt

Setting

Message

Protagonist

Name

Driving Goal

Obstacle or Conflict

Get writing!

Word Count ______

Title

Themes

Prompt

Setting

Message

Protagonist

Name

Driving Goal

Obstacle or Conflict

Get writing!

Word Count

Title

Themes

Prompt

Setting

Message

Protagonist

Name

Driving Goal

Obstacle or Conflict

Get writing!

Word Count

Title

Themes

Prompt

Setting

Message

Protagonist

Name

Driving Goal

Obstacle or Conflict

Get writing!

Word Count

Title

Themes

Prompt

Setting

Message

Protagonist

Name

Driving Goal

Obstacle or Conflict

Get writing!

Word Count

Title

Themes

Prompt

Setting

Message

Protagonist

Name

Driving Goal

Obstacle or Conflict

Get writing!

Word Count

Title

Themes

Prompt

Setting

Message

Protagonist

Name

Driving Goal

Obstacle or Conflict

Get writing!

Word Count

Title

Themes

Prompt

Setting

Message

Protagonist

Name

Driving Goal

Obstacle or Conflict

Get writing!

Word Count

Title

Themes

Prompt

Setting

Message

Protagonist

Name

Driving Goal

Obstacle or Conflict

Get writing!

Word Count

Title

Themes

Prompt

Setting

Message

Protagonist

Name

Driving Goal

Obstacle or Conflict

Get writing!

Word Count

Title

Themes

Prompt

Setting

Message

Protagonist

Name

Driving Goal

Obstacle or Conflict

Get writing!

Word Count

Title

Themes

Prompt

Setting

Message

Protagonist

Name

Driving Goal

Obstacle or Conflict

Get writing!

Word Count

Title

Themes

Prompt

Setting

Message

Protagonist

Name

Driving Goal

Obstacle or Conflict

Get writing!

Word Count

Title

Themes

Prompt

Setting

Message

Protagonist

Name

Driving Goal

Obstacle or Conflict

Get writing!

Word Count

Title

Themes

Prompt

Setting

Message

Protagonist

Name

Driving Goal

Obstacle or Conflict

Get writing!

Word Count

Title

Themes

Prompt

Setting

Message

Protagonist

Name

Driving Goal

Obstacle or Conflict

Get writing!

Word Count

Title

Themes

Prompt

Setting

Message

Protagonist

Name

Driving Goal

Obstacle or Conflict

Get writing!

Word Count

Title

Themes

Prompt

Setting

Message

Protagonist

Name

Driving Goal

Obstacle or Conflict

Get writing!

Word Count

Title

Themes

Prompt

Setting

Message

Protagonist

Name

Driving Goal

Obstacle or Conflict

Get writing!

Word Count

Title

Themes

Prompt

Setting

Message

Protagonist

Name

Driving Goal

Obstacle or Conflict

Get writing!

Word Count

Title

Themes

Prompt

Setting

Message

Protagonist

Name

Driving Goal

Obstacle or Conflict

Get writing!

Word Count ____________

Title

Themes

Prompt

Setting

Message

Protagonist

Name

Driving Goal

Obstacle or Conflict

Get writing!

Word Count

Title

Themes

Prompt

Setting

Message

Protagonist

Name

Driving Goal

Obstacle or Conflict

Get writing!

Word Count

Title

Themes

Prompt

Setting

Message

Protagonist

Name

Driving Goal

Obstacle or Conflict

Get writing!

Word Count

Title

Themes

Prompt

Setting

Message

Protagonist

Name

Driving Goal

Obstacle or Conflict

Get writing!

Word Count

Title

Themes

Prompt

Setting

Message

Protagonist

Name

Driving Goal

Obstacle or Conflict

Get writing!

Word Count ________

Title

Themes

Prompt

Setting

Message

Protagonist

Name

Driving Goal

Obstacle or Conflict

Get writing!

Word Count

Title

Themes

Prompt

Setting

Message

Protagonist

Name

Driving Goal

Obstacle or Conflict

Get writing!

Word Count

Title

Themes

Prompt

Setting

Message

Protagonist

Name

Driving Goal

Obstacle or Conflict

Get writing!

Word Count

Title

Themes

Prompt

Setting

Message

Protagonist

Name

Driving Goal

Obstacle or Conflict

Get writing!

Word Count

Title

Themes

Prompt

Setting

Message

Protagonist

Name

Driving Goal

Obstacle or Conflict

Get writing!

Word Count

Title

Themes

Prompt

Setting

Message

Protagonist

Name

Driving Goal

Obstacle or Conflict

Get writing!

Word Count

Title

Themes

Prompt

Setting

Message

Protagonist

Name

Driving Goal

Obstacle or Conflict

Get writing!

Word Count

Title

Themes

Prompt

Setting

Message

Protagonist

Name

Driving Goal

Obstacle or Conflict

Get writing!

Word Count

Title

Themes

Prompt

Setting

Message

Protagonist

Name

Driving Goal

Obstacle or Conflict

Get writing!

Word Count

Title

Themes

Prompt

Setting

Message

Protagonist

Name

Driving Goal

Obstacle or Conflict

Get writing!

Word Count

Title

Themes

Prompt

Setting

Message

Protagonist

Name

Driving Goal

Obstacle or Conflict

Get writing!

Word Count

Title

Themes

Prompt

Setting

Message

Protagonist

Name

Driving Goal

Obstacle or Conflict

Get writing!

Word Count

Title

Themes

Prompt

Setting

Message

Protagonist

Name

Driving Goal

Obstacle or Conflict

Get writing!

Word Count

Title

Themes

Prompt

Setting

Message

Protagonist

Name

Driving Goal

Obstacle or Conflict

Get writing!

Word Count

Title

Themes

Prompt

Setting

Message

Protagonist

Name

Driving Goal

Obstacle or Conflict

Get writing!

Word Count

Title

Themes

Prompt

Setting

Message

Protagonist

Name

Driving Goal

Obstacle or Conflict

Get writing!

Word Count

Title

Themes

Prompt

Setting

Message

Protagonist

Name

Driving Goal

Obstacle or Conflict

Get writing!

Word Count

Title

Themes

Prompt

Setting

Message

Protagonist

Name

Driving Goal

Obstacle or Conflict

Get writing!

Word Count

Title

Themes

Prompt

Setting

Message

Protagonist

Name

Driving Goal

Obstacle or Conflict

Get writing!

Word Count

Title

Themes

Prompt

Setting

Message

Protagonist

Name

Driving Goal

Obstacle or Conflict

Get writing!

Word Count

Title

Themes

Prompt

Setting

Message

Protagonist

Name

Driving Goal

Obstacle or Conflict

Get writing!

Word Count ______

Title

Themes

Prompt

Setting

Message

Protagonist

Name

Driving Goal

Obstacle or Conflict

Get writing!

Word Count

Title

Themes

Prompt

Setting

Message

Protagonist

Name

Driving Goal

Obstacle or Conflict

Get writing!

Word Count

Title

Themes

Prompt

Setting

Message

Protagonist

Name

Driving Goal

Obstacle or Conflict

Get writing!

Word Count ______

Title

Themes

Prompt

Setting

Message

Protagonist

Name

Driving Goal

Obstacle or Conflict

Get writing!

Word Count

Title

Themes

Prompt

Setting

Message

Protagonist

Name

Driving Goal

Obstacle or Conflict

Get writing!

Word Count ____________

Title

Themes

Prompt

Setting

Message

Protagonist

Name

Driving Goal

Obstacle or Conflict

Get writing!

Word Count

Title

Themes

Prompt

Setting

Message

Protagonist

Name

Driving Goal

Obstacle or Conflict

Get writing!

Word Count

Title

Themes

Prompt

Setting

Message

Protagonist

Name

Driving Goal

Obstacle or Conflict

Get writing!

Word Count

Title

Themes

Prompt

Setting

Message

Protagonist

Name

Driving Goal

Obstacle or Conflict

Get writing!

Word Count

Title

Themes

Prompt

Setting

Message

Protagonist

Name

Driving Goal

Obstacle or Conflict

Get writing!

Word Count

Title

Themes

Prompt

Setting

Message

Protagonist

Name

Driving Goal

Obstacle or Conflict

Get writing!

Word Count

Title

Themes

Prompt

Setting

Message

Protagonist

Name

Driving Goal

Obstacle or Conflict

Get writing!

Word Count

Title

Themes

Prompt

Setting

Message

Protagonist

Name

Driving Goal

Obstacle or Conflict

Get writing!

Word Count

Title

Themes

Prompt

Setting

Message

Protagonist

Name

Driving Goal

Obstacle or Conflict

Get writing!

Word Count

Title

Themes

Prompt

Setting

Message

Protagonist

Name

Driving Goal

Obstacle or Conflict

Get writing!

Word Count

Title

Themes

Prompt

Setting

Message

Protagonist

Name

Driving Goal

Obstacle or Conflict

Get writing!

Word Count

Title

Themes

Prompt

Setting

Message

Protagonist

Name

Driving Goal

Obstacle or Conflict

Get writing!

Word Count

Title

Themes

Prompt

Setting

Message

Protagonist

Name

Driving Goal

Obstacle or Conflict

Get writing!

Word Count

Title

Themes

Prompt

Setting

Message

Protagonist

Name

Driving Goal

Obstacle or Conflict

Get writing!

Word Count

Title

Themes

Prompt

Setting

Message

Protagonist

Name

Driving Goal

Obstacle or Conflict

Get writing!

Word Count

Title

Themes

Prompt

Setting

Message

Protagonist

Name

Driving Goal

Obstacle or Conflict

Get writing!

Word Count

Title

Themes

Prompt

Setting

Message

Protagonist

Name

Driving Goal

Obstacle or Conflict

Get writing!

Word Count

Title

Themes

Prompt

Setting

Message

Protagonist

Name

Driving Goal

Obstacle or Conflict

Get writing!

Word Count ____________

Title

Themes

Prompt

Setting

Message

Protagonist

Name

Driving Goal

Obstacle or Conflict

Get writing!

Word Count

Title

Themes

Prompt

Setting

Message

Protagonist

Name

Driving Goal

Obstacle or Conflict

Get writing!

Word Count

Title

Themes

Prompt

Setting

Message

Protagonist

Name

Driving Goal

Obstacle or Conflict

Get writing!

Word Count

Title

Themes

Prompt

Setting

Message

Protagonist

Name

Driving Goal

Obstacle or Conflict

Get writing!

Word Count

Title

Themes

Prompt

Setting

Message

Protagonist

Name

Driving Goal

Obstacle or Conflict

Get writing!

Word Count

Title

Themes

Prompt

Setting

Message

Protagonist

Name

Driving Goal

Obstacle or Conflict

Get writing!

Word Count

Title

Themes

Prompt

Setting

Message

Protagonist

Name

Driving Goal

Obstacle or Conflict

Get writing!

Word Count

Title

Themes

Prompt

Setting

Message

Protagonist

Name

Driving Goal

Obstacle or Conflict

Get writing!

Word Count

Title

Themes

Prompt

Setting

Message

Protagonist

Name

Driving Goal

Obstacle or Conflict

Get writing!

Word Count

Title

Themes

Prompt

Setting

Message

Protagonist

Name

Driving Goal

Obstacle or Conflict

Get writing!

Word Count

Title

Themes

Prompt

Setting

Message

Protagonist

Name

Driving Goal

Obstacle or Conflict

Get writing!

Word Count

Title

Themes

Prompt

Setting

Message

Protagonist

Name

Driving Goal

Obstacle or Conflict

Get writing!

Word Count

Title

Themes

Prompt

Setting

Message

Protagonist

Name

Driving Goal

Obstacle or Conflict

Get writing!

Word Count

Title

Themes

Prompt

Setting

Message

Protagonist

Name

Driving Goal

Obstacle or Conflict

Get writing!

Word Count

Title

Themes

Prompt

Setting

Message

Protagonist

Name

Driving Goal

Obstacle or Conflict

Get writing!

Word Count

Title

Themes

Prompt

Setting

Message

Protagonist

Name

Driving Goal

Obstacle or Conflict

Get writing!

Word Count

Title

Themes

Prompt

Setting

Message

Protagonist

Name

Driving Goal

Obstacle or Conflict

Get writing!

Word Count

Title

Themes

Prompt

Setting

Message

Protagonist

Name

Driving Goal

Obstacle or Conflict

Get writing!

Word Count

Title

Themes

Prompt

Setting

Message

Protagonist

Name

Driving Goal

Obstacle or Conflict

Get writing!

Word Count ______________

Title

Themes

Prompt

Setting

Message

Protagonist

Name

Driving Goal

Obstacle or Conflict

Get writing!

Word Count

Title

Themes

Prompt

Setting

Message

Protagonist

Name

Driving Goal

Obstacle or Conflict

Get writing!

Word Count ______________

Title

Themes

Prompt

Setting

Message

Protagonist

Name

Driving Goal

Obstacle or Conflict

Get writing!

Word Count

Title

Themes

Prompt

Setting

Message

Protagonist

Name

Driving Goal

Obstacle or Conflict

Get writing!

Word Count

Title

Themes

Prompt

Setting

Message

Protagonist

Name

Driving Goal

Obstacle or Conflict

Get writing!

Word Count

Title

Themes

Prompt

Setting

Message

Protagonist

Name

Driving Goal

Obstacle or Conflict

Get writing!

Word Count

Title

Themes

Prompt

Setting

Message

Protagonist

Name

Driving Goal

Obstacle or Conflict

Get writing!

Word Count ____________

Title

Themes

Prompt

Setting

Message

Protagonist

Name

Driving Goal

Obstacle or Conflict

Get writing!

Word Count

Title

Themes

Prompt

Setting

Message

Protagonist

Name

Driving Goal

Obstacle or Conflict

Get writing!

Word Count

Title

Themes

Prompt

Setting

Message

Protagonist

Name

Driving Goal

Obstacle or Conflict

Get writing!

Word Count

Title

Themes

Prompt

Setting

Message

Protagonist

Name

Driving Goal

Obstacle or Conflict

Get writing!

Word Count

Title

Themes

Prompt

Setting

Message

Protagonist

Name

Driving Goal

Obstacle or Conflict

Get writing!

Word Count

Title

Themes

Prompt

Setting

Message

Protagonist

Name

Driving Goal

Obstacle or Conflict

Get writing!

Word Count

Title

Themes

Prompt

Setting

Message

Protagonist

Name

Driving Goal

Obstacle or Conflict

Get writing!

Word Count

Title

Themes

Prompt

Setting

Message

Protagonist

Name

Driving Goal

Obstacle or Conflict

Get writing!

Word Count

Title

Themes

Prompt

Setting

Message

Protagonist

Name

Driving Goal

Obstacle or Conflict

Get writing!

Word Count

Title

Themes

Prompt

Setting

Message

Protagonist

Name

Driving Goal

Obstacle or Conflict

Get writing!

Word Count

Title

Themes

Prompt

Setting

Message

Protagonist

Name

Driving Goal

Obstacle or Conflict

Get writing!

Word Count

Title

Themes

Prompt

Setting

Message

Protagonist

Name

Driving Goal

Obstacle or Conflict

Get writing!

Word Count ________

Title

Themes

Prompt

Setting

Message

Protagonist

Name

Driving Goal

Obstacle or Conflict

Get writing!

Word Count

Title

Themes

Prompt

Setting

Message

Protagonist

Name

Driving Goal

Obstacle or Conflict

Get writing!

Word Count

Title

Themes

Prompt

Setting

Message

Protagonist

Name

Driving Goal

Obstacle or Conflict

Get writing!

Word Count

Title

Themes

Prompt

Setting

Message

Protagonist

Name

Driving Goal

Obstacle or Conflict

Get writing!

Word Count

Title

Themes

Prompt

Setting

Message

Protagonist

Name

Driving Goal

Obstacle or Conflict

Get writing!

Word Count

Title

Themes

Prompt

Setting

Message

Protagonist

Name

Driving Goal

Obstacle or Conflict

Get writing!

Word Count

Title

Themes

Prompt

Setting

Message

Protagonist

Name

Driving Goal

Obstacle or Conflict

Get writing!

Word Count

Title

Themes

Prompt

Setting

Message

Protagonist

Name

Driving Goal

Obstacle or Conflict

Get writing!

Word Count

Title

Themes

Prompt

Setting

Message

Protagonist

Name

Driving Goal

Obstacle or Conflict

Get writing!

Word Count

Title

Themes

Prompt

Setting

Message

Protagonist

Name

Driving Goal

Obstacle or Conflict

Get writing!

Word Count

Title

Themes

Prompt

Setting

Message

Protagonist

Name

Driving Goal

Obstacle or Conflict

Get writing!

Word Count

Title

Themes

Prompt

Setting

Message

Protagonist

Name

Driving Goal

Obstacle or Conflict

Get writing!

Word Count

Title

Themes

Prompt

Setting

Message

Protagonist

Name

Driving Goal

Obstacle or Conflict

Get writing!

Word Count

Title

Themes

Prompt

Setting

Message

Protagonist

Name

Driving Goal

Obstacle or Conflict

Get writing!

Word Count ______

Title

Themes

Prompt

Setting

Message

Protagonist

Name

Driving Goal

Obstacle or Conflict

Get writing!

Word Count

Title

Themes

Prompt

Setting

Message

Protagonist

Name

Driving Goal

Obstacle or Conflict

Get writing!

Word Count ____________

Title

Themes

Prompt

Setting

Message

Protagonist

Name

Driving Goal

Obstacle or Conflict

Get writing!

Word Count

Title

Themes

Prompt

Setting

Message

Protagonist

Name

Driving Goal

Obstacle or Conflict

Get writing!

Word Count

Title

Themes

Prompt

Setting

Message

Protagonist

Name

Driving Goal

Obstacle or Conflict

Get writing!

Word Count

Title

Themes

Prompt

Setting

Message

Protagonist

Name

Driving Goal

Obstacle or Conflict

Get writing!

Word Count

Title

Themes

Prompt

Setting

Message

Protagonist

Name

Driving Goal

Obstacle or Conflict

Get writing!

Word Count

Title

Themes

Prompt

Setting

Message

Protagonist

Name

Driving Goal

Obstacle or Conflict

Get writing!

Word Count

Title

Themes

Prompt

Setting

Message

Protagonist

Name

Driving Goal

Obstacle or Conflict

Get writing!

Word Count

Title

Themes

Prompt

Setting

Message

Protagonist

Name

Driving Goal

Obstacle or Conflict

Get writing!

Word Count

Title

Themes

Prompt

Setting

Message

Protagonist

Name

Driving Goal

Obstacle or Conflict

Get writing!

Word Count

Title

Themes

Prompt

Setting

Message

Protagonist

Name

Driving Goal

Obstacle or Conflict

Get writing!

Word Count

Title

Themes

Prompt

Setting

Message

Protagonist

Name

Driving Goal

Obstacle or Conflict

Get writing!

Word Count

Title

Themes

Prompt

Setting

Message

Protagonist

Name

Driving Goal

Obstacle or Conflict

Get writing!

Word Count

Title

Themes

Prompt

Setting

Message

Protagonist

Name

Driving Goal

Obstacle or Conflict

Get writing!

Word Count

Title

Themes

Prompt

Setting

Message

Protagonist

Name

Driving Goal

Obstacle or Conflict

Get writing!

Word Count

Title

Themes

Prompt

Setting

Message

Protagonist

Name

Driving Goal

Obstacle or Conflict

Get writing!

Word Count

Title

Themes

Prompt

Setting

Message

Protagonist

Name

Driving Goal

Obstacle or Conflict

Get writing!

Word Count

Title

Themes

Prompt

Setting

Message

Protagonist

Name

Driving Goal

Obstacle or Conflict

Get writing!

Word Count

Title

Themes

Prompt

Setting

Message

Protagonist

Name

Driving Goal

Obstacle or Conflict

Get writing!

Word Count

Title

Themes

Prompt

Setting

Message

Protagonist

Name

Driving Goal

Obstacle or Conflict

Get writing!

Word Count

Title

Themes

Prompt

Setting

Message

Protagonist

Name

Driving Goal

Obstacle or Conflict

Get writing!

Word Count

Title

Themes

Prompt

Setting

Message

Protagonist

Name

Driving Goal

Obstacle or Conflict

Get writing!

Word Count

Title

Themes

Prompt

Setting

Message

Protagonist

Name

Driving Goal

Obstacle or Conflict

Get writing!

Word Count

Title

Themes

Prompt

Setting

Message

Protagonist

Name

Driving Goal

Obstacle or Conflict

Get writing!

Word Count

Title

Themes

Prompt

Setting

Message

Protagonist

Name

Driving Goal

Obstacle or Conflict

Get writing!

Word Count

Title

Themes

Prompt

Setting

Message

Protagonist

Name

Driving Goal

Obstacle or Conflict

Get writing!

Word Count

Title

Themes

Prompt

Setting

Message

Protagonist

Name

Driving Goal

Obstacle or Conflict

Get writing!

Word Count

Title

Themes

Prompt

Setting

Message

Protagonist

Name

Driving Goal

Obstacle or Conflict

Get writing!

Word Count

Title

Themes

Prompt

Setting

Message

Protagonist

Name

Driving Goal

Obstacle or Conflict

Get writing!

Word Count

Title

Themes

Prompt

Setting

Message

Protagonist

Name

Driving Goal

Obstacle or Conflict

Get writing!

Word Count

Title

Themes

Prompt

Setting

Message

Protagonist

Name

Driving Goal

Obstacle or Conflict

Get writing!

Word Count ____________

Title

Themes

Prompt

Setting

Message

Protagonist

Name

Driving Goal

Obstacle or Conflict

Get writing!

Word Count

Title

Themes

Prompt

Setting

Message

Protagonist

Name

Driving Goal

Obstacle or Conflict

Get writing!

Word Count

Title

Themes

Prompt

Setting

Message

Protagonist

Name

Driving Goal

Obstacle or Conflict

Get writing!

Word Count ____________

Title

Themes

Prompt

Setting

Message

Protagonist

Name

Driving Goal

Obstacle or Conflict

Get writing!

Word Count

Title

Themes

Prompt

Setting

Message

Protagonist

Name

Driving Goal

Obstacle or Conflict

Get writing!

Word Count

Title

Themes

Prompt

Setting

Message

Protagonist

Name

Driving Goal

Obstacle or Conflict

Get writing!

Word Count

Title

Themes

Prompt

Setting

Message

Protagonist

Name

Driving Goal

Obstacle or Conflict

Get writing!

Word Count ____________

Title

Themes

Prompt

Setting

Message

Protagonist

Name

Driving Goal

Obstacle or Conflict

Get writing!

Word Count

Title

Themes

Prompt

Setting

Message

Protagonist

Name

Driving Goal

Obstacle or Conflict

Get writing!

Word Count

Title

Themes

Prompt

Setting

Message

Protagonist

Name

Driving Goal

Obstacle or Conflict

Get writing!

Word Count

Title

Themes

Prompt

Setting

Message

Protagonist

Name

Driving Goal

Obstacle or Conflict

Get writing!

Word Count

Title

Themes

Prompt

Setting

Message

Protagonist

Name

Driving Goal

Obstacle or Conflict

Get writing!

Word Count ____________

Title

Themes

Prompt

Setting

Message

Protagonist

Name

Driving Goal

Obstacle or Conflict

Get writing!

Word Count

Title

Themes

Prompt

Setting

Message

Protagonist

Name

Driving Goal

Obstacle or Conflict

Get writing!

Word Count ______

Title

Themes

Prompt

Setting

Message

Protagonist

Name

Driving Goal

Obstacle or Conflict

Get writing!

Word Count

Title

Themes

Prompt

Setting

Message

Protagonist

Name

Driving Goal

Obstacle or Conflict

Get writing!

Word Count ____________

Title

Themes

Prompt

Setting

Message

Protagonist

Name

Driving Goal

Obstacle or Conflict

Get writing!

Word Count

Title

Themes

Prompt

Setting

Message

Protagonist

Name

Driving Goal

Obstacle or Conflict

Get writing!

Word Count

Title

Themes

Prompt

Setting

Message

Protagonist

Name

Driving Goal

Obstacle or Conflict

Get writing!

Word Count

Title

Themes

Prompt

Setting

Message

Protagonist

Name

Driving Goal

Obstacle or Conflict

Get writing!

Word Count

Title

Themes

Prompt

Setting

Message

Protagonist

Name

Driving Goal

Obstacle or Conflict

Get writing!

Word Count

Title

Themes

Prompt

Setting

Message

Protagonist

Name

Driving Goal

Obstacle or Conflict

Get writing!

Word Count

Title

Themes

Prompt

Setting

Message

Protagonist

Name

Driving Goal

Obstacle or Conflict

Get writing!

Word Count

Title

Themes

Prompt

Setting

Message

Protagonist

Name

Driving Goal

Obstacle or Conflict

Get writing!

Word Count

Title

Themes

Prompt

Setting

Message

Protagonist

Name

Driving Goal

Obstacle or Conflict

Get writing!

Word Count ______

Title

Themes

Prompt

Setting

Message

Protagonist

Name

Driving Goal

Obstacle or Conflict

Get writing!

Word Count

Title

Themes

Prompt

Setting

Message

Protagonist

Name

Driving Goal

Obstacle or Conflict

Get writing!

Word Count

Title

Themes

Prompt

Setting

Message

Protagonist

Name

Driving Goal

Obstacle or Conflict

Get writing!

Word Count ____________

Title

Themes

Prompt

Setting

Message

Protagonist

Name

Driving Goal

Obstacle or Conflict

Get writing!

Word Count

Title

Themes

Prompt

Setting

Message

Protagonist

Name

Driving Goal

Obstacle or Conflict

Get writing!

Word Count

Title

Themes

Prompt

Setting

Message

Protagonist

Name

Driving Goal

Obstacle or Conflict

Get writing!

Word Count ______

Title

Themes

Prompt

Setting

Message

Protagonist

Name

Driving Goal

Obstacle or Conflict

Get writing!

Word Count

Title

Themes

Prompt

Setting

Message

Protagonist

Name

Driving Goal

Obstacle or Conflict

Get writing!

Word Count

Title

Themes

Prompt

Setting

Message

Protagonist

Name

Driving Goal

Obstacle or Conflict

Get writing!

Word Count

Title

Themes

Prompt

Setting

Message

Protagonist

Name

Driving Goal

Obstacle or Conflict

Get writing!

Word Count

Title

Themes

Prompt

Setting

Message

Protagonist

Name

Driving Goal

Obstacle or Conflict

Get writing!

Word Count

Title

Themes

Prompt

Setting

Message

Protagonist

Name

Driving Goal

Obstacle or Conflict

Get writing!

Word Count

Title

Themes

Prompt

Setting

Message

Protagonist

Name

Driving Goal

Obstacle or Conflict

Get writing!

Word Count

Title

Themes

Prompt

Setting

Message

Protagonist

Name

Driving Goal

Obstacle or Conflict

Get writing!

Word Count

Title

Themes

Prompt

Setting

Message

Protagonist

Name

Driving Goal

Obstacle or Conflict

Get writing!

Word Count ______

Title

Themes

Prompt

Setting

Message

Protagonist

Name

Driving Goal

Obstacle or Conflict

Get writing!

Word Count

Title

Themes

Prompt

Setting

Message

Protagonist

Name

Driving Goal

Obstacle or Conflict

Get writing!

Word Count

Title

Themes

Prompt

Setting

Message

Protagonist

Name

Driving Goal

Obstacle or Conflict

Get writing!

Word Count

Title

Themes

Prompt

Setting

Message

Protagonist

Name

Driving Goal

Obstacle or Conflict

Get writing!

Word Count

Title

Themes

Prompt

Setting

Message

Protagonist

Name

Driving Goal

Obstacle or Conflict

Get writing!

Word Count

Title

Themes

Prompt

Setting

Message

Protagonist

Name

Driving Goal

Obstacle or Conflict

Get writing!

Word Count

Title

Themes

Prompt

Setting

Message

Protagonist

Name

Driving Goal

Obstacle or Conflict

Get writing!

Word Count

Title

Themes

Prompt

Setting

Message

Protagonist

Name

Driving Goal

Obstacle or Conflict

Get writing!

Word Count ______

Title

Themes

Prompt

Setting

Message

Protagonist

Name

Driving Goal

Obstacle or Conflict

Get writing!

Word Count

Title

Themes

Prompt

Setting

Message

Protagonist

Name

Driving Goal

Obstacle or Conflict

Get writing!

Word Count

Title

Themes

Prompt

Setting

Message

Protagonist

Name

Driving Goal

Obstacle or Conflict

Get writing!

Word Count

Title

Themes

Prompt

Setting

Message

Protagonist

Name

Driving Goal

Obstacle or Conflict

Get writing!

Word Count

Title

Themes

Prompt

Setting

Message

Protagonist

Name

Driving Goal

Obstacle or Conflict

Get writing!

Word Count

Title

Themes

Prompt

Setting

Message

Protagonist

Name

Driving Goal

Obstacle or Conflict

Get writing!

Word Count ____________

Title

Themes

Prompt

Setting

Message

Protagonist

Name

Driving Goal

Obstacle or Conflict

Get writing!

Word Count

Title

Themes

Prompt

Setting

Message

Protagonist

Name

Driving Goal

Obstacle or Conflict

Get writing!

Word Count

Title

Themes

Prompt

Setting

Message

Protagonist

Name

Driving Goal

Obstacle or Conflict

Get writing!

Word Count

Title

Themes

Prompt

Setting

Message

Protagonist

Name

Driving Goal

Obstacle or Conflict

Get writing!

Word Count

Title

Themes

Prompt

Setting

Message

Protagonist

Name

Driving Goal

Obstacle or Conflict

Get writing!

Word Count

Title

Themes

Prompt

Setting

Message

Protagonist

Name

Driving Goal

Obstacle or Conflict

Get writing!

Word Count

Title

Themes

Prompt

Setting

Message

Protagonist

Name

Driving Goal

Obstacle or Conflict

Get writing!

Word Count

Title

Themes

Prompt

Setting

Message

Protagonist

Name

Driving Goal

Obstacle or Conflict

Get writing!

Word Count

Title

Themes

Prompt

Setting

Message

Protagonist

Name

Driving Goal

Obstacle or Conflict

Get writing!

Word Count

Title

Themes

Prompt

Setting

Message

Protagonist

Name

Driving Goal

Obstacle or Conflict

Get writing!

Word Count

Title

Themes

Prompt

Setting

Message

Protagonist

Name

Driving Goal

Obstacle or Conflict

Get writing!

Word Count

Title

Themes

Prompt

Setting

Message

Protagonist

Name

Driving Goal

Obstacle or Conflict

Get writing!

Word Count

Title

Themes

Prompt

Setting

Message

Protagonist

Name

Driving Goal

Obstacle or Conflict

Get writing!

Word Count

Title

Themes

Prompt

Setting

Message

Protagonist

Name

Driving Goal

Obstacle or Conflict

Get writing!

Word Count

Title

Themes

Prompt

Setting

Message

Protagonist

Name

Driving Goal

Obstacle or Conflict

Get writing!

Word Count

Title

Themes

Prompt

Setting

Message

Protagonist

Name

Driving Goal

Obstacle or Conflict

Get writing!

Word Count

Title

Themes

Prompt

Setting

Message

Protagonist

Name

Driving Goal

Obstacle or Conflict

Get writing!

Word Count

Title

Themes

Prompt

Setting

Message

Protagonist

Name

Driving Goal

Obstacle or Conflict

Get writing!

Word Count

Title

Themes

Prompt

Setting

Message

Protagonist

Name

Driving Goal

Obstacle or Conflict

Get writing!

Word Count

Title

Themes

Prompt

Setting

Message

Protagonist

Name

Driving Goal

Obstacle or Conflict

Get writing!

Word Count

Title

Themes

Prompt

Setting

Message

Protagonist

Name

Driving Goal

Obstacle or Conflict

Get writing!

Word Count

Title

Themes

Prompt

Setting

Message

Protagonist

Name

Driving Goal

Obstacle or Conflict

Get writing!

Word Count

Title

Themes

Prompt

Setting

Message

Protagonist

Name

Driving Goal

Obstacle or Conflict

Get writing!

Word Count

Title

Themes

Prompt

Setting

Message

Protagonist

Name

Driving Goal

Obstacle or Conflict

Get writing!

Word Count

Title

Themes

Prompt

Setting

Message

Protagonist

Name

Driving Goal

Obstacle or Conflict

Get writing!

Word Count

Title

Themes

Prompt

Setting

Message

Protagonist

Name

Driving Goal

Obstacle or Conflict

Get writing!

Word Count

Title

Themes

Prompt

Setting

Message

Protagonist

Name

Driving Goal

Obstacle or Conflict

Get writing!

Word Count

Title

Themes

Prompt

Setting

Message

Protagonist

Name

Driving Goal

Obstacle or Conflict

Get writing!

Word Count

Title

Themes

Prompt

Setting

Message

Protagonist

Name

Driving Goal

Obstacle or Conflict

Get writing!

Word Count

Title

Themes

Prompt

Setting

Message

Protagonist

Name

Driving Goal

Obstacle or Conflict

Get writing!

Word Count

Title

Themes

Prompt

Setting

Message

Protagonist

Name

Driving Goal

Obstacle or Conflict

Get writing!

Word Count

Title

Themes

Prompt

Setting

Message

Protagonist

Name

Driving Goal

Obstacle or Conflict

Get writing!

Word Count

Title

Themes

Prompt

Setting

Message

Protagonist

Name

Driving Goal

Obstacle or Conflict

Get writing!

Word Count

Title

Themes

Prompt

Setting

Message

Protagonist

Name

Driving Goal

Obstacle or Conflict

Get writing!

Word Count

Title

Themes

Prompt

Setting

Message

Protagonist

Name

Driving Goal

Obstacle or Conflict

Get writing!

Word Count

Title

Themes

Prompt

Setting

Message

Protagonist

Name

Driving Goal

Obstacle or Conflict

Get writing!

Word Count ______

Title

Themes

Prompt

Setting

Message

Protagonist

Name

Driving Goal

Obstacle or Conflict

Get writing!

Word Count

Title

Themes

Prompt

Setting

Message

Protagonist

Name

Driving Goal

Obstacle or Conflict

Get writing!

Word Count

Title

Themes

Prompt

Setting

Message

Protagonist

Name

Driving Goal

Obstacle or Conflict

Get writing!

Word Count

Title

Themes

Prompt

Setting

Message

Protagonist

Name

Driving Goal

Obstacle or Conflict

Get writing!

Word Count

Title

Themes

Prompt

Setting

Message

Protagonist

Name

Driving Goal

Obstacle or Conflict

Get writing!

Word Count

Title

Themes

Prompt

Setting

Message

Protagonist

Name

Driving Goal

Obstacle or Conflict

Get writing!

Word Count

Title

Themes

Prompt

Setting

Message

Protagonist

Name

Driving Goal

Obstacle or Conflict

Get writing!

Word Count

Title

Themes

Prompt

Setting

Message

Protagonist

Name

Driving Goal

Obstacle or Conflict

Get writing!

Word Count

Title

Themes

Prompt

Setting

Message

Protagonist

Name

Driving Goal

Obstacle or Conflict

Get writing!

Word Count

Title

Themes

Prompt

Setting

Message

Protagonist

Name

Driving Goal

Obstacle or Conflict

Get writing!

Word Count

Title

Themes

Prompt

Setting

Message

Protagonist

Name

Driving Goal

Obstacle or Conflict

Get writing!

Word Count ______________

Title

Themes

Prompt

Setting

Message

Protagonist

Name

Driving Goal

Obstacle or Conflict

Get writing!

Word Count

Title

Themes

Prompt

Setting

Message

Protagonist

Name

Driving Goal

Obstacle or Conflict

Get writing!

Word Count

Title

Themes

Prompt

Setting

Message

Protagonist

Name

Driving Goal

Obstacle or Conflict

Get writing!

Word Count

Title

Themes

Prompt

Setting

Message

Protagonist

Name

Driving Goal

Obstacle or Conflict

Get writing!

Word Count

Title

Themes

Prompt

Setting

Message

Protagonist

Name

Driving Goal

Obstacle or Conflict

Get writing!

Word Count

Title

Themes

Prompt

Setting

Message

Protagonist

Name

Driving Goal

Obstacle or Conflict

Get writing!

Word Count

Title

Themes

Prompt

Setting

Message

Protagonist

Name

Driving Goal

Obstacle or Conflict

Get writing!

Word Count

Title

Themes

Prompt

Setting

Message

Protagonist

Name

Driving Goal

Obstacle or Conflict

Get writing!

Word Count

Title

Themes

Prompt

Setting

Message

Protagonist

Name

Driving Goal

Obstacle or Conflict

Get writing!

Word Count

Title

Themes

Prompt

Setting

Message

Protagonist

Name

Driving Goal

Obstacle or Conflict

Get writing!

Word Count

Title

Themes

Prompt

Setting

Message

Protagonist

Name

Driving Goal

Obstacle or Conflict

Get writing!

Word Count

Title

Themes

Prompt

Setting

Message

Protagonist

Name

Driving Goal

Obstacle or Conflict

Get writing!

Word Count

Title

Themes

Prompt

Setting

Message

Protagonist

Name

Driving Goal

Obstacle or Conflict

Get writing!

Word Count

Title

Themes

Prompt

Setting

Message

Protagonist

Name

Driving Goal

Obstacle or Conflict

Get writing!

Word Count

Title

Themes

Prompt

Setting

Message

Protagonist

Name

Driving Goal

Obstacle or Conflict

Get writing!

Word Count

Title

Themes

Prompt

Setting

Message

Protagonist

Name

Driving Goal

Obstacle or Conflict

Get writing!

Word Count

Title

Themes

Prompt

Setting

Message

Protagonist

Name

Driving Goal

Obstacle or Conflict

Get writing!

Word Count

Title

Themes

Prompt

Setting

Message

Protagonist

Name

Driving Goal

Obstacle or Conflict

Get writing!

Word Count

Title

Themes

Prompt

Setting

Message

Protagonist

Name

Driving Goal

Obstacle or Conflict

Get writing!

Word Count

Title

Themes

Prompt

Setting

Message

Protagonist

Name

Driving Goal

Obstacle or Conflict

Get writing!

Word Count

Title

Themes

Prompt

Setting

Message

Protagonist

Name

Driving Goal

Obstacle or Conflict

Get writing!

Word Count

Title

Themes

Prompt

Setting

Message

Protagonist

Name

Driving Goal

Obstacle or Conflict

Get writing!

Word Count

Title

Themes

Prompt

Setting

Message

Protagonist

Name

Driving Goal

Obstacle or Conflict

Get writing!

Word Count

Title

Themes

Prompt

Setting

Message

Protagonist

Name

Driving Goal

Obstacle or Conflict

Get writing!

Word Count

Title

Themes

Prompt

Setting

Message

Protagonist

Name

Driving Goal

Obstacle or Conflict

Get writing!

Word Count

Title

Themes

Prompt

Setting

Message

Protagonist

Name

Driving Goal

Obstacle or Conflict

Get writing!

Word Count

Title

Themes

Prompt

Setting

Message

Protagonist

Name

Driving Goal

Obstacle or Conflict

Get writing!

Word Count

Title

Themes

Prompt

Setting

Message

Protagonist

Name

Driving Goal

Obstacle or Conflict

Get writing!

Word Count

Title

Themes

Prompt

Setting

Message

Protagonist

Name

Driving Goal

Obstacle or Conflict

Get writing!

Word Count

Title

Themes

Prompt

Setting

Message

Protagonist

Name

Driving Goal

Obstacle or Conflict

Get writing!

Word Count

Title

Themes

Prompt

Setting

Message

Protagonist

Name

Driving Goal

Obstacle or Conflict

Get writing!

Word Count ____________

Title

Themes

Prompt

Setting

Message

Protagonist

Name

Driving Goal

Obstacle or Conflict

Get writing!

Word Count

Title

Themes

Prompt

Setting

Message

Protagonist

Name

Driving Goal

Obstacle or Conflict

Get writing!

Word Count

Title

Themes

Prompt

Setting

Message

Protagonist

Name

Driving Goal

Obstacle or Conflict

Get writing!

Word Count

Title

Themes

Prompt

Setting

Message

Protagonist

Name

Driving Goal

Obstacle or Conflict

Get writing!

Word Count

Title

Themes

Prompt

Setting

Message

Protagonist

Name

Driving Goal

Obstacle or Conflict

Get writing!

Word Count

Title

Themes

Prompt

Setting

Message

Protagonist

Name

Driving Goal

Obstacle or Conflict

Get writing!

Word Count

Title

Themes

Prompt

Setting

Message

Protagonist

Name

Driving Goal

Obstacle or Conflict

Get writing!

Word Count

Title

Themes

Prompt

Setting

Message

Protagonist

Name

Driving Goal

Obstacle or Conflict

Get writing!

Word Count

Title

Themes

Prompt

Setting

Message

Protagonist

Name

Driving Goal

Obstacle or Conflict

Get writing!

Word Count

Title

Themes

Prompt

Setting

Message

Protagonist

Name

Driving Goal

Obstacle or Conflict

Get writing!

Word Count

Title

Themes

Prompt

Setting

Message

Protagonist

Name

Driving Goal

Obstacle or Conflict

Get writing!

Word Count

Title

Themes

Prompt

Setting

Message

Protagonist

Name

Driving Goal

Obstacle or Conflict

Get writing!

Word Count

Title

Themes

Prompt

Setting

Message

Protagonist

Name

Driving Goal

Obstacle or Conflict

Get writing!

Word Count

Title

Themes

Prompt

Setting

Message

Protagonist

Name

Driving Goal

Obstacle or Conflict

Get writing!

Word Count

Title

Themes

Prompt

Setting

Message

Protagonist

Name

Driving Goal

Obstacle or Conflict

Get writing!

Word Count

Title

Themes

Prompt

Setting

Message

Protagonist

Name

Driving Goal

Obstacle or Conflict

Get writing!

Word Count

Title

Themes

Prompt

Setting

Message

Protagonist

Name

Driving Goal

Obstacle or Conflict

Get writing!

Word Count

Title

Themes

Prompt

Setting

Message

Protagonist

Name

Driving Goal

Obstacle or Conflict

Get writing!

Word Count

Title

Themes

Prompt

Setting

Message

Protagonist

Name

Driving Goal

Obstacle or Conflict

Get writing!

Word Count

Title

Themes

Prompt

Setting

Message

Protagonist

Name

Driving Goal

Obstacle or Conflict

Get writing!

Word Count

Title

Themes

Prompt

Setting

Message

Protagonist

Name

Driving Goal

Obstacle or Conflict

Get writing!

Word Count

Title

Themes

Prompt

Setting

Message

Protagonist

Name

Driving Goal

Obstacle or Conflict

Get writing!

Word Count

Title

Themes

Prompt

Setting

Message

Protagonist

Name

Driving Goal

Obstacle or Conflict

Get writing!

Word Count

Title

Themes

Prompt

Setting

Message

Protagonist

Name

Driving Goal

Obstacle or Conflict

Get writing!

Word Count

Title

Themes

Prompt

Setting

Message

Protagonist

Name

Driving Goal

Obstacle or Conflict

Get writing!

Word Count

Title

Themes

Prompt

Setting

Message

Protagonist

Name

Driving Goal

Obstacle or Conflict

Get writing!

Word Count

Title

Themes

Prompt

Setting

Message

Protagonist

Name

Driving Goal

Obstacle or Conflict

Get writing!

Word Count

Title

Themes

Prompt

Setting

Message

Protagonist

Name

Driving Goal

Obstacle or Conflict

Get writing!

Word Count

Title

Themes

Prompt

Setting

Message

Protagonist

Name

Driving Goal

Obstacle or Conflict

Get writing!

Word Count

Title

Themes

Prompt

Setting

Message

Protagonist

Name

Driving Goal

Obstacle or Conflict

Get writing!

Word Count

Title

Themes

Prompt

Setting

Message

Protagonist

Name

Driving Goal

Obstacle or Conflict

Get writing!

Word Count

Title

Themes

Prompt

Setting

Message

Protagonist

Name

Driving Goal

Obstacle or Conflict

Get writing!

Word Count ____________

Title

Themes

Prompt

Setting

Message

Protagonist

Name

Driving Goal

Obstacle or Conflict

Get writing!

Word Count

Title

Themes

Prompt

Setting

Message

Protagonist

Name

Driving Goal

Obstacle or Conflict

Get writing!

Word Count

Title

Themes

Prompt

Setting

Message

Protagonist

Name

Driving Goal

Obstacle or Conflict

Get writing!

Word Count

Title

Themes

Prompt

Setting

Message

Protagonist

Name

Driving Goal

Obstacle or Conflict

Get writing!

Word Count ____________

Title

Themes

Prompt

Setting

Message

Protagonist

Name

Driving Goal

Obstacle or Conflict

Get writing!

Word Count

Title

Themes

Prompt

Setting

Message

Protagonist

Name

Driving Goal

Obstacle or Conflict

Get writing!

Word Count

Title

Themes

Prompt

Setting

Message

Protagonist

Name

Driving Goal

Obstacle or Conflict

Get writing!

Word Count

Title

Themes

Prompt

Setting

Message

Protagonist

Name

Driving Goal

Obstacle or Conflict

Get writing!

Word Count

Title

Themes

Prompt

Setting

Message

Protagonist

Name

Driving Goal

Obstacle or Conflict

Get writing!

Word Count

Title

Themes

Prompt

Setting

Message

Protagonist

Name

Driving Goal

Obstacle or Conflict

Get writing!

Word Count

Title

Themes

Prompt

Setting

Message

Protagonist

Name

Driving Goal

Obstacle or Conflict

Get writing!

Word Count

Title

Themes

Prompt

Setting

Message

Protagonist

Name

Driving Goal

Obstacle or Conflict

Get writing!

Word Count

Title

Themes

Prompt

Setting

Message

Protagonist

Name

Driving Goal

Obstacle or Conflict

Get writing!

Word Count

Title

Themes

Prompt

Setting

Message

Protagonist

Name

Driving Goal

Obstacle or Conflict

Get writing!

Word Count

Title

Themes

Prompt

Setting

Message

Protagonist

Name

Driving Goal

Obstacle or Conflict

Get writing!

Word Count

Title

Themes

Prompt

Setting

Message

Protagonist

Name

Driving Goal

Obstacle or Conflict

Get writing!

Word Count

Title

Themes

Prompt

Setting

Message

Protagonist

Name

Driving Goal

Obstacle or Conflict

Get writing!

Word Count ______

Title

Themes

Prompt

Setting

Message

Protagonist

Name

Driving Goal

Obstacle or Conflict

Get writing!

Word Count

Title

Themes

Prompt

Setting

Message

Protagonist

Name

Driving Goal

Obstacle or Conflict

Get writing!

Word Count

Title

Themes

Prompt

Setting

Message

Protagonist

Name

Driving Goal

Obstacle or Conflict

Get writing!

Word Count

Title

Themes

Prompt

Setting

Message

Protagonist

Name

Driving Goal

Obstacle or Conflict

Get writing!

Word Count

Title

Themes

Prompt

Setting

Message

Protagonist

Name

Driving Goal

Obstacle or Conflict

Get writing!

Word Count

Title

Themes

Prompt

Setting

Message

Protagonist

Name

Driving Goal

Obstacle or Conflict

Get writing!

Word Count

Title

Themes

Prompt

Setting

Message

Protagonist

Name

Driving Goal

Obstacle or Conflict

Get writing!

Word Count

Title

Themes

Prompt

Setting

Message

Protagonist

Name

Driving Goal

Obstacle or Conflict

Get writing!

Word Count

Title

Themes

Prompt

Setting

Message

Protagonist

Name

Driving Goal

Obstacle or Conflict

Get writing!

Word Count

Title

Themes

Prompt

Setting

Message

Protagonist

Name

Driving Goal

Obstacle or Conflict

Get writing!

Word Count

Title

Themes

Prompt

Setting

Message

Protagonist

Name

Driving Goal

Obstacle or Conflict

Get writing!

Word Count

Title

Themes

Prompt

Setting

Message

Protagonist

Name

Driving Goal

Obstacle or Conflict

Get writing!

Word Count

Title

Themes

Prompt

Setting

Message

Protagonist

Name

Driving Goal

Obstacle or Conflict

Get writing!

Word Count

Title

Themes

Prompt

Setting

Message

Protagonist

Name

Driving Goal

Obstacle or Conflict

Get writing!

Word Count

Title

Themes

Prompt

Setting

Message

Protagonist

Name

Driving Goal

Obstacle or Conflict

Get writing!

Word Count

Title

Themes

Prompt

Setting

Message

Protagonist

Name

Driving Goal

Obstacle or Conflict

Get writing!

Word Count

Title

Themes

Prompt

Setting

Message

Protagonist

Name

Driving Goal

Obstacle or Conflict

Get writing!

Word Count

Title

Themes

Prompt

Setting

Message

Protagonist

Name

Driving Goal

Obstacle or Conflict

Get writing!

Word Count

Title

Themes

Prompt

Setting

Message

Protagonist

Name

Driving Goal

Obstacle or Conflict

Get writing!

Word Count ____________

Title

Themes

Prompt

Setting

Message

Protagonist

Name

Driving Goal

Obstacle or Conflict

Get writing!

Word Count

Title

Themes

Prompt

Setting

Message

Protagonist

Name

Driving Goal

Obstacle or Conflict

Get writing!

Word Count

Title

Themes

Prompt

Setting

Message

Protagonist

Name

Driving Goal

Obstacle or Conflict

Get writing!

Word Count

Title

Themes

Prompt

Setting

Message

Protagonist

Name

Driving Goal

Obstacle or Conflict

Get writing!

Word Count ____________

Title

Themes

Prompt

Setting

Message

Protagonist

Name

Driving Goal

Obstacle or Conflict

Get writing!

Word Count ______________

Title

Themes

Prompt

Setting

Message

Protagonist

Name

Driving Goal

Obstacle or Conflict

Get writing!

Word Count

Title

Themes

Prompt

Setting

Message

Protagonist

Name

Driving Goal

Obstacle or Conflict

Get writing!

Word Count

Title

Themes

Prompt

Setting

Message

Protagonist

Name

Driving Goal

Obstacle or Conflict

Get writing!

Word Count

Title

Themes

Prompt

Setting

Message

Protagonist

Name

Driving Goal

Obstacle or Conflict

Get writing!

Word Count

Title

Themes

Prompt

Setting

Message

Protagonist

Name

Driving Goal

Obstacle or Conflict

Get writing!

Word Count ____________

Title

Themes

Prompt

Setting

Message

Protagonist

Name

Driving Goal

Obstacle or Conflict

Get writing!

Word Count

Title

Themes

Prompt

Setting

Message

Protagonist

Name

Driving Goal

Obstacle or Conflict

Get writing!

Word Count

Title

Themes

Prompt

Setting

Message

Protagonist

Name

Driving Goal

Obstacle or Conflict

Get writing!

Word Count

Title

Themes

Prompt

Setting

Message

Protagonist

Name

Driving Goal

Obstacle or Conflict

Get writing!

Word Count

Title

Themes

Prompt

Setting

Message

Protagonist

Name

Driving Goal

Obstacle or Conflict

Get writing!

Word Count

Title

Themes

Prompt

Setting

Message

Protagonist

Name

Driving Goal

Obstacle or Conflict

Get writing!

Word Count

Title

Themes

Prompt

Setting

Message

Protagonist

Name

Driving Goal

Obstacle or Conflict

Get writing!

Word Count

Title

Themes

Prompt

Setting

Message

Protagonist

Name

Driving Goal

Obstacle or Conflict

Get writing!

Word Count

Title

Themes

Prompt

Setting

Message

Protagonist

Name

Driving Goal

Obstacle or Conflict

Get writing!

Word Count

Title

Themes

Prompt

Setting

Message

Protagonist

Name

Driving Goal

Obstacle or Conflict

Get writing!

Word Count

Title

Themes

Prompt

Setting

Message

Protagonist

Name

Driving Goal

Obstacle or Conflict

Get writing!

Word Count

Title

Themes

Prompt

Setting

Message

Protagonist

Name

Driving Goal

Obstacle or Conflict

Get writing!

Word Count

Title

Themes

Prompt

Setting

Message

Protagonist

Name

Driving Goal

Obstacle or Conflict

Get writing!

Word Count

Title

Themes

Prompt

Setting

Message

Protagonist

Name

Driving Goal

Obstacle or Conflict

Get writing!

Word Count

Title

Themes

Prompt

Setting

Message

Protagonist

Name

Driving Goal

Obstacle or Conflict

Get writing!

Word Count

Title

Themes

Prompt

Setting

Message

Protagonist

Name

Driving Goal

Obstacle or Conflict

Get writing!

Word Count

Title

Themes

Prompt

Setting

Message

Protagonist

Name

Driving Goal

Obstacle or Conflict

Get writing!

Word Count

Title

Themes

Prompt

Setting

Message

Protagonist

Name

Driving Goal

Obstacle or Conflict

Get writing!

Word Count

Title

Themes

Prompt

Setting

Message

Protagonist

Name

Driving Goal

Obstacle or Conflict

Get writing!

Word Count

Title

Themes

Prompt

Setting

Message

Protagonist

Name

Driving Goal

Obstacle or Conflict

Get writing!

Word Count

Title

Themes

Prompt

Setting

Message

Protagonist

Name

Driving Goal

Obstacle or Conflict

Get writing!

Word Count

Title

Themes

Prompt

Setting

Message

Protagonist

Name

Driving Goal

Obstacle or Conflict

Get writing!

Word Count

Title

Themes

Prompt

Setting

Message

Protagonist

Name

Driving Goal

Obstacle or Conflict

Get writing!

Word Count

Title

Themes

Prompt

Setting

Message

Protagonist

Name

Driving Goal

Obstacle or Conflict

Get writing!

Word Count

Title

Themes

Prompt

Setting

Message

Protagonist

Name

Driving Goal

Obstacle or Conflict

Get writing!

Word Count

Title

Themes

Prompt

Setting

Message

Protagonist

Name

Driving Goal

Obstacle or Conflict

Get writing!

Word Count

Title

Themes

Prompt

Setting

Message

Protagonist

Name

Driving Goal

Obstacle or Conflict

Get writing!

Word Count

Title

Themes

Prompt

Setting

Message

Protagonist

Name

Driving Goal

Obstacle or Conflict

Get writing!

Word Count

Title

Themes

Prompt

Setting

Message

Protagonist

Name

Driving Goal

Obstacle or Conflict

Get writing!

Word Count

Title

Themes

Prompt

Setting

Message

Protagonist

Name

Driving Goal

Obstacle or Conflict

Get writing!

Word Count

Title

Themes

Prompt

Setting

Message

Protagonist

Name

Driving Goal

Obstacle or Conflict

Get writing!

Word Count

Title

Themes

Prompt

Setting

Message

Protagonist

Name

Driving Goal

Obstacle or Conflict

Get writing!

Word Count

Title

Themes

Prompt

Setting

Message

Protagonist

Name

Driving Goal

Obstacle or Conflict

Get writing!

Word Count

Title

Themes

Prompt

Setting

Message

Protagonist

Name

Driving Goal

Obstacle or Conflict

Get writing!

Word Count

Title

Themes

Prompt

Setting

Message

Protagonist

Name

Driving Goal

Obstacle or Conflict

Get writing!

Word Count

Title

Themes

Prompt

Setting

Message

Protagonist

Name

Driving Goal

Obstacle or Conflict

Get writing!

Word Count ______

Title

Themes

Prompt

Setting

Message

Protagonist

Name

Driving Goal

Obstacle or Conflict

Get writing!

Word Count

Title

Themes

Prompt

Setting

Message

Protagonist

Name

Driving Goal

Obstacle or Conflict

Get writing!

Word Count

Title

Themes

Prompt

Setting

Message

Protagonist

Name

Driving Goal

Obstacle or Conflict

Get writing!

Word Count

Title

Themes

Prompt

Setting

Message

Protagonist

Name

Driving Goal

Obstacle or Conflict

Get writing!

Word Count

Title

Themes

Prompt

Setting

Message

Protagonist

Name

Driving Goal

Obstacle or Conflict

Get writing!

Word Count

Title

Themes

Prompt

Setting

Message

Protagonist

Name

Driving Goal

Obstacle or Conflict

Get writing!

Word Count

Title

Themes

Prompt

Setting

Message

Protagonist

Name

Driving Goal

Obstacle or Conflict

Get writing!

Word Count

Title

Themes

Prompt

Setting

Message

Protagonist

Name

Driving Goal

Obstacle or Conflict

Get writing!

Word Count

Title

Themes

Prompt

Setting

Message

Protagonist

Name

Driving Goal

Obstacle or Conflict

Get writing!

Word Count

Title

Themes

Prompt

Setting

Message

Protagonist

Name

Driving Goal

Obstacle or Conflict

Get writing!

Word Count

Title

Themes

Prompt

Setting

Message

Protagonist

Name

Driving Goal

Obstacle or Conflict

Get writing!

Word Count

Title

Themes

Prompt

Setting

Message

Protagonist

Name

Driving Goal

Obstacle or Conflict

Get writing!

Word Count ______________

Title

Themes

Prompt

Setting

Message

Protagonist

Name

Driving Goal

Obstacle or Conflict

Get writing!

Word Count

Title

Themes

Prompt

Setting

Message

Protagonist

Name

Driving Goal

Obstacle or Conflict

Get writing!

Word Count

Title

Themes

Prompt

Setting

Message

Protagonist

Name

Driving Goal

Obstacle or Conflict

Get writing!

Word Count

Title

Themes

Prompt

Setting

Message

Protagonist

Name

Driving Goal

Obstacle or Conflict

Get writing!

Word Count

Title

Themes

Prompt

Setting

Message

Protagonist

Name

Driving Goal

Obstacle or Conflict

Get writing!

Word Count

Title

Themes

Prompt

Setting

Message

Protagonist

Name

Driving Goal

Obstacle or Conflict

Get writing!

Word Count ____________

Title

Themes

Prompt

Setting

Message

Protagonist

Name

Driving Goal

Obstacle or Conflict

Get writing!

Word Count ____________

Title

Themes

Prompt

Setting

Message

Protagonist

Name

Driving Goal

Obstacle or Conflict

Get writing!

Word Count

Title

Themes

Prompt

Setting

Message

Protagonist

Name

Driving Goal

Obstacle or Conflict

Get writing!

Word Count ______________

Title

Themes

Prompt

Setting

Message

Protagonist

Name

Driving Goal

Obstacle or Conflict

Get writing!

Word Count

Title

Themes

Prompt

Setting

Message

Protagonist

Name

Driving Goal

Obstacle or Conflict

Get writing!

Word Count

Title

Themes

Prompt

Setting

Message

Protagonist

Name

Driving Goal

Obstacle or Conflict

Get writing!

Word Count

Title

Themes

Prompt

Setting

Message

Protagonist

Name

Driving Goal

Obstacle or Conflict

Get writing!

Word Count

Title

Themes

Prompt

Setting

Message

Protagonist

Name

Driving Goal

Obstacle or Conflict

Get writing!

Word Count

Title

Themes

Prompt

Setting

Message

Protagonist

Name

Driving Goal

Obstacle or Conflict

Get writing!

Word Count

Title

Themes

Prompt

Setting

Message

Protagonist

Name

Driving Goal

Obstacle or Conflict

Get writing!

Word Count ____________

Title

Themes

Prompt

Setting

Message

Protagonist

Name

Driving Goal

Obstacle or Conflict

Get writing!

Word Count

Title

Themes

Prompt

Setting

Message

Protagonist

Name

Driving Goal

Obstacle or Conflict

Get writing!

Word Count

Title

Themes

Prompt

Setting

Message

Protagonist

Name

Driving Goal

Obstacle or Conflict

Get writing!

Word Count

Title

Themes

Prompt

Setting

Message

Protagonist

Name

Driving Goal

Obstacle or Conflict

Get writing!

Word Count

Title

Themes

Prompt

Setting

Message

Protagonist

Name

Driving Goal

Obstacle or Conflict

Get writing!

Word Count

Title

Themes

Prompt

Setting

Message

Protagonist

Name

Driving Goal

Obstacle or Conflict

Get writing!

Word Count

Title

Themes

Prompt

Setting

Message

Protagonist

Name

Driving Goal

Obstacle or Conflict

Get writing!

Word Count

Title

Themes

Prompt

Setting

Message

Protagonist

Name

Driving Goal

Obstacle or Conflict

Get writing!

Word Count

Title

Themes

Prompt

Setting

Message

Protagonist

Name

Driving Goal

Obstacle or Conflict

Get writing!

Word Count

www.ingramcontent.com/pod-product-compliance
Lightning Source LLC
Chambersburg PA
CBHW081333090726
47907CB00011B/2463

* 9 7 8 1 6 4 9 4 4 3 2 6 7 *